Just Look 'n Learn
ENGLISH
PICTURE DICTIONARY

1,500 Words for Beginning English Learners

Learn to Tell Time– Learn to Count

Illustrations and Example Sentences for Each Entry

Illustrated by
Daniel J. Hochstatter

McGraw·Hill

New York Chicago San Francisco Lisbon London Madrid Mexico City
Milan New Delhi San Juan Seoul Singapore Sydney Toronto

423.1
Jus

Who is in this book?

Thomas

Aunt Alice

Uncle Edward

Mary

Susan

Mother and Father

Grandfather and Grandmother

Robert

Helen

Jimmy

William

Steven

The McGraw·Hill Companies

Library of Congress Cataloging-in-Publication Data

Just Look 'n Learn English picture dictionary / illustrated by Daniel J. Hochstatter.
        p.   cm.
    Includes index.
    ISBN 0-07-140833-9
    1. Picture dictionaries, English.   I. Hochstatter, Daniel J.
PC1629.J87   1996
423'.1—dc20
                                            96-21070
                                            CIP

1 2 3 4 5 6 7 8 9 0   WKT/WKT   1 0 9 8 7 6 5 4 3 2

ISBN 0-07-140833-9

McGraw-Hill books are available at special quantity discounts to use as premiums and sales
promotions, or for use in corporate training programs. For more information, please write to the
Director of Special Sales, Professional Publishing, McGraw-Hill, Two Penn Plaza, New York, NY
10121-2298. Or contact your local bookstore.

This book is printed on acid-free paper

What is in this book?

The *Words and Pictures* start on the next page.

There are many *Numbers* to learn on pages **82**, **83**, **84**, and **85**.

Learn the *Days of the Week* on pages **86** and **87**.

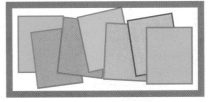

See the names of the *Months* on pages **88** and **89**.

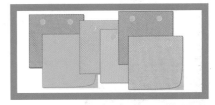

The names of different *Shapes* are on pages **90** and **91**.

Learn about *Compass Directions* on pages **92** and **93**.

Try telling *Time* on page **94**.

When you see an ✱ in the dictionary, look for the *Irregular English Words* on page **95**.

Aa*Aa***Aa***Aa*

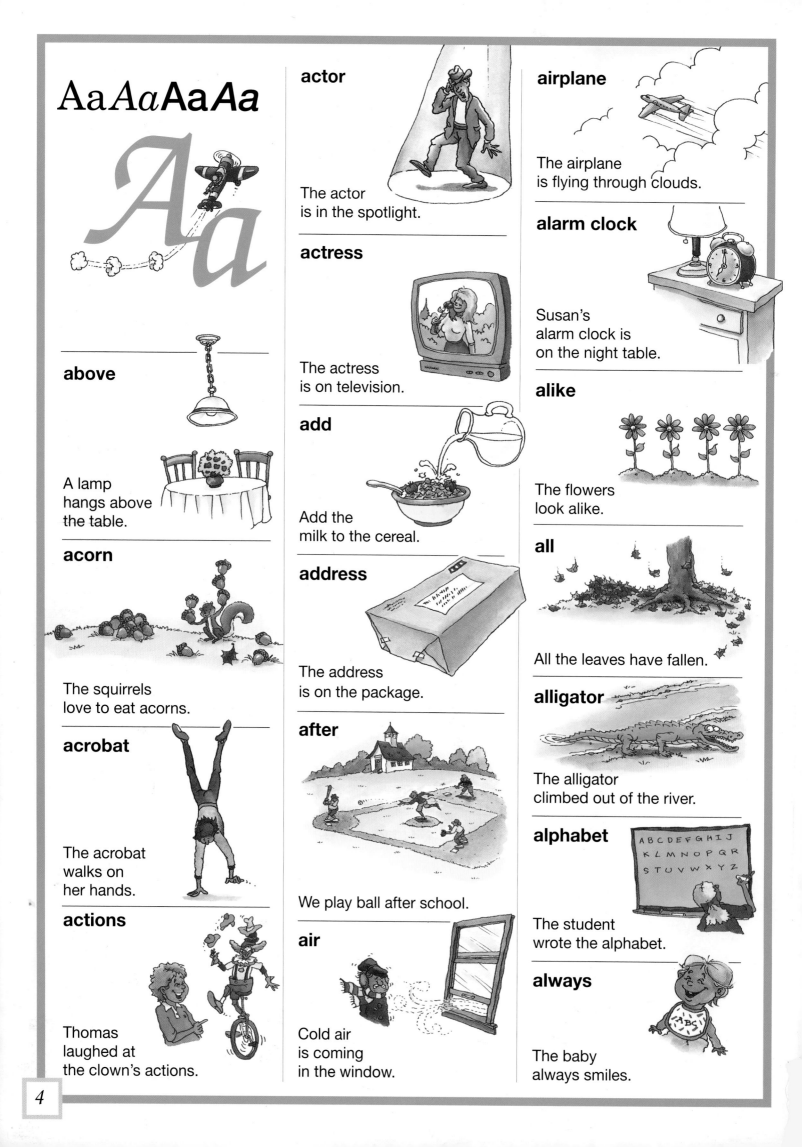

above

A lamp hangs above the table.

acorn

The squirrels love to eat acorns.

acrobat

The acrobat walks on her hands.

actions

Thomas laughed at the clown's actions.

actor

The actor is in the spotlight.

actress

The actress is on television.

add

Add the milk to the cereal.

address

The address is on the package.

after

We play ball after school.

air

Cold air is coming in the window.

airplane

The airplane is flying through clouds.

alarm clock

Susan's alarm clock is on the night table.

alike

The flowers look alike.

all

All the leaves have fallen.

alligator

The alligator climbed out of the river.

alphabet

The student wrote the alphabet.

always

The baby always smiles.

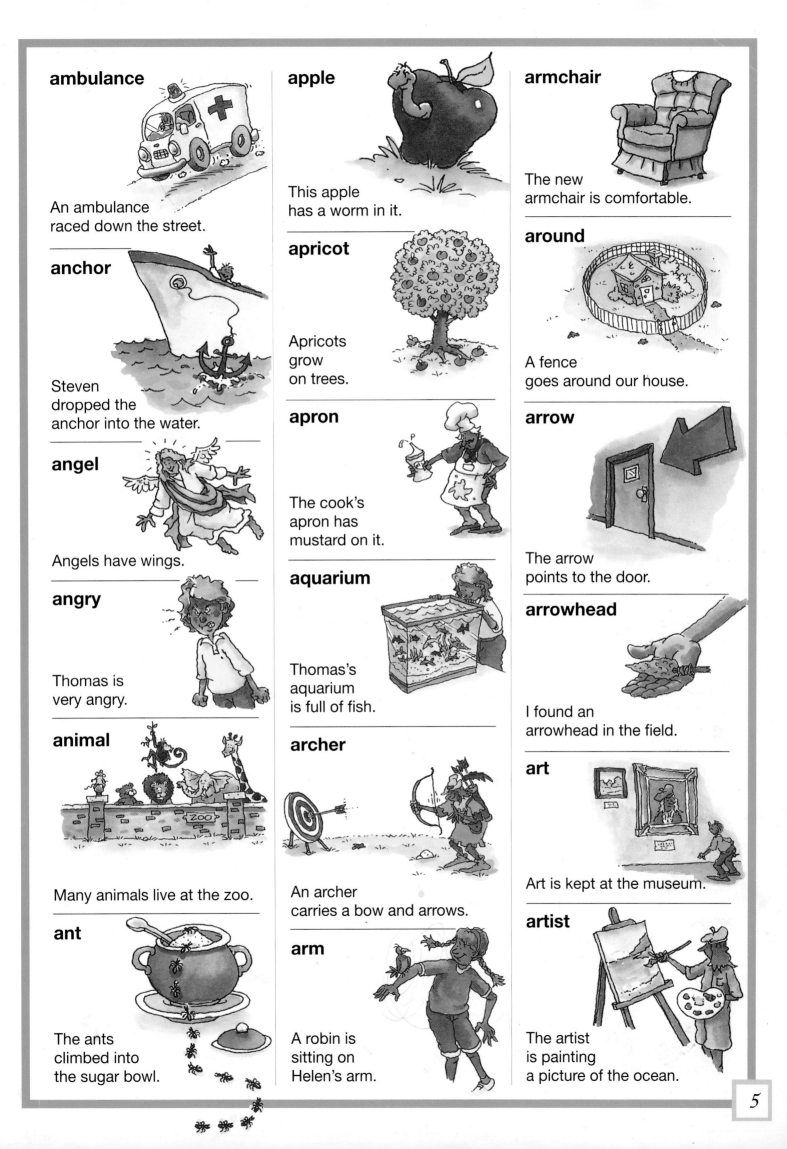

ambulance

An ambulance raced down the street.

anchor

Steven dropped the anchor into the water.

angel

Angels have wings.

angry

Thomas is very angry.

animal

Many animals live at the zoo.

ant

The ants climbed into the sugar bowl.

apple

This apple has a worm in it.

apricot

Apricots grow on trees.

apron

The cook's apron has mustard on it.

aquarium

Thomas's aquarium is full of fish.

archer

An archer carries a bow and arrows.

arm

A robin is sitting on Helen's arm.

armchair

The new armchair is comfortable.

around

A fence goes around our house.

arrow

The arrow points to the door.

arrowhead

I found an arrowhead in the field.

art

Art is kept at the museum.

artist

The artist is painting a picture of the ocean.

astronaut

The astronaut stood on the moon.

at

Jimmy is at home all day.

athlete

The athlete won a gold medal.

attic

Grandma's house has an attic.

aunt

Thomas's aunt is his father's sister.

autumn

In the autumn we rake leaves.

avocado

Mary ate an avocado for lunch.

away

The rabbit ran away.

ax

The farmer is cutting the tree down with an ax.

BbBbBbBb

baby

The baby is playing with toys.

back

Susan has a zipper on the back of her dress.

backpack

Many students wear backpacks to school.

bad

The weather was too bad for a picnic.

badminton

We played badminton in the yard.

bag

William puts an apple into his lunch bag.

baggage

Our baggage was heavy!

bake

My mom baked some bread for me.

baker

The baker is happy.

bakery

Uncle Edward buys bread at the bakery.

ball

My new ball is on the roof.

balloon

The boy's balloon is tied to his wrist.

banana

I have bananas with my cereal.

band

The band is playing in the park.

bandage

Robert has a bandage on his cut.

bang

The balloon made a loud bang.

bangs

Helen's bangs hang down over her forehead.

bank

I take my money to the bank.

banner

I held a red and gold banner in the parade.

barbecue

He cooked chicken on the barbecue.

barbecue

Uncle Edward barbecued a chicken for dinner.

barber

The barber's scissors are sharp.

barn

The farmer keeps his cows in the barn.

barrel

I could drink a barrel of lemonade!

barrette

Mary wears a barrette in her long hair.

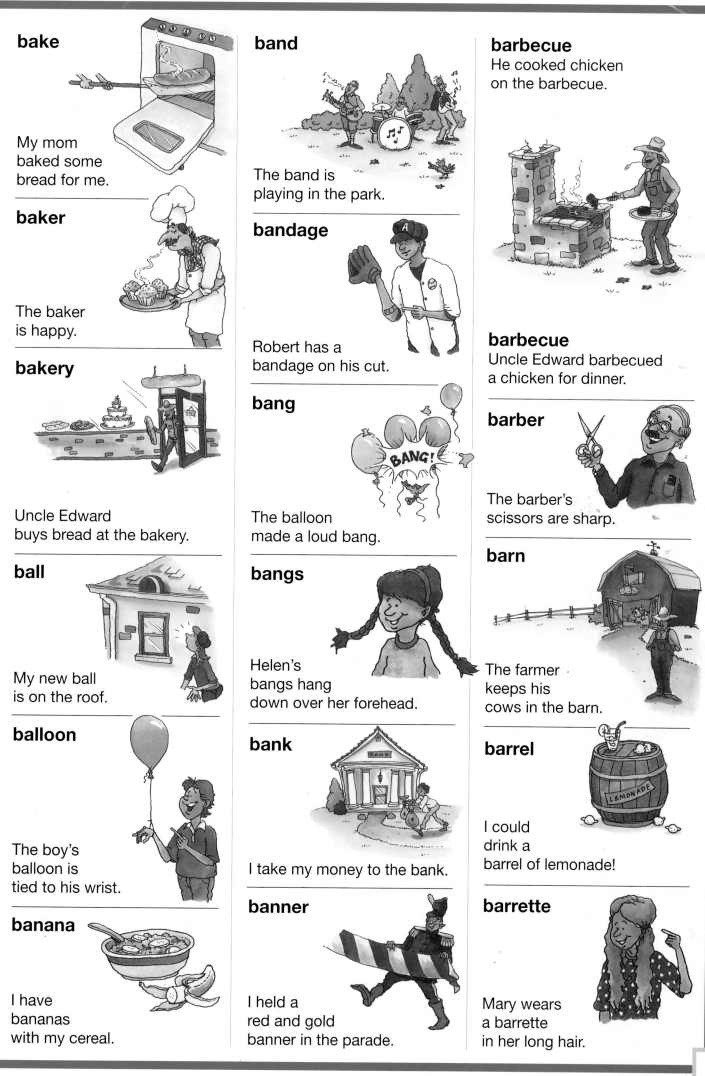

baseball

William caught the baseball.

basket

The basket is full of eggs.

basketball

The students are playing basketball.

bat

Bats live in the cave.

bat

Robert hit the baseball with his new bat.

bath

Jimmy is taking a bath.

bathe

Mother bathes baby Jimmy often.

bathing suit

My bathing suit is green.

bathrobe

My mom has an old, purple bathrobe.

bathroom

The bathroom is clean.

bathtub

The children played in the bathtub.

bay

The boats in the bay are safe.

be*

You will be tall soon.

beach

White sand covers the beach.

beak

A bird eats with its beak.

bear

A brown bear ran out of the forest.

bear cub

The bear cubs climbed a tree.

8

beard

Steven's grandfather has a long, gray beard.

beautiful

Susan's party dress is beautiful.

beaver

The beaver has a flat tail.

become*

Susan is becoming tall.

bed

My bed is too soft.

bedroom

Mary's bedroom has two beds in it.

bee

Bees make honey.

behind

The tall boy stood behind his brother.

bell

Steven rings the bell for dinner.

below

Water runs below the bridge.

belt

Steven's belt is too wide for his pants.

bench

The dog is sleeping on the bench.

beneath

My bed is beneath my brother's.

beside

The dog sat beside my chair.

best*

The best athlete wins a prize.

better*

Susan is a better runner than William.

between

My aunt is sitting between me and my sister.

bicycle

Susan often rides her bicycle to school.

big

This is a big cake!

big top

A circus tent is called a big top.

bill

The bird's bill is orange.

bill

Thomas found a five-dollar bill.

binoculars

Robert is looking through the binoculars.

bird

The bird sat in the tree.

birthday

My brother had a party on his birthday.

birthday cake

My birthday cake has candles on it.

bite*

Stop biting your fingernails.

bite

Will you give me a bite?

black

My father wears a black suit to work.

blackboard

Helen will clean the blackboard.

blanket

My blanket keeps me warm.

block

I walk three blocks to school.

block

My little sister plays with blocks.

blossom

The tree has red blossoms.

blouse

I have a blouse to go with my skirt.

blow*

The wind blew our kite around the sky.

blue

The butterfly is blue.

blush

Helen blushed when her name was called.

board

The farmer sawed boards to fix the fence.

boat

William sailed his boat on the pond.

body

You wash your body in the bathtub.

bone

The dog carried the bone to his house.

book

Steven is reading a book.

bookcase

The bookcase is full.

boot

I wear boots when it snows.

both

Both apples are red.

bottle

Medicine comes in a bottle.

bottom

William opened the bottom drawer.

boulder

A boulder fell near the car.

bouquet

I gave Grandma a big bouquet of flowers.

bow

Steven is bowing to the audience.

bow

There was a large bow on the package.

bowl

Thomas ate a bowl of cereal.

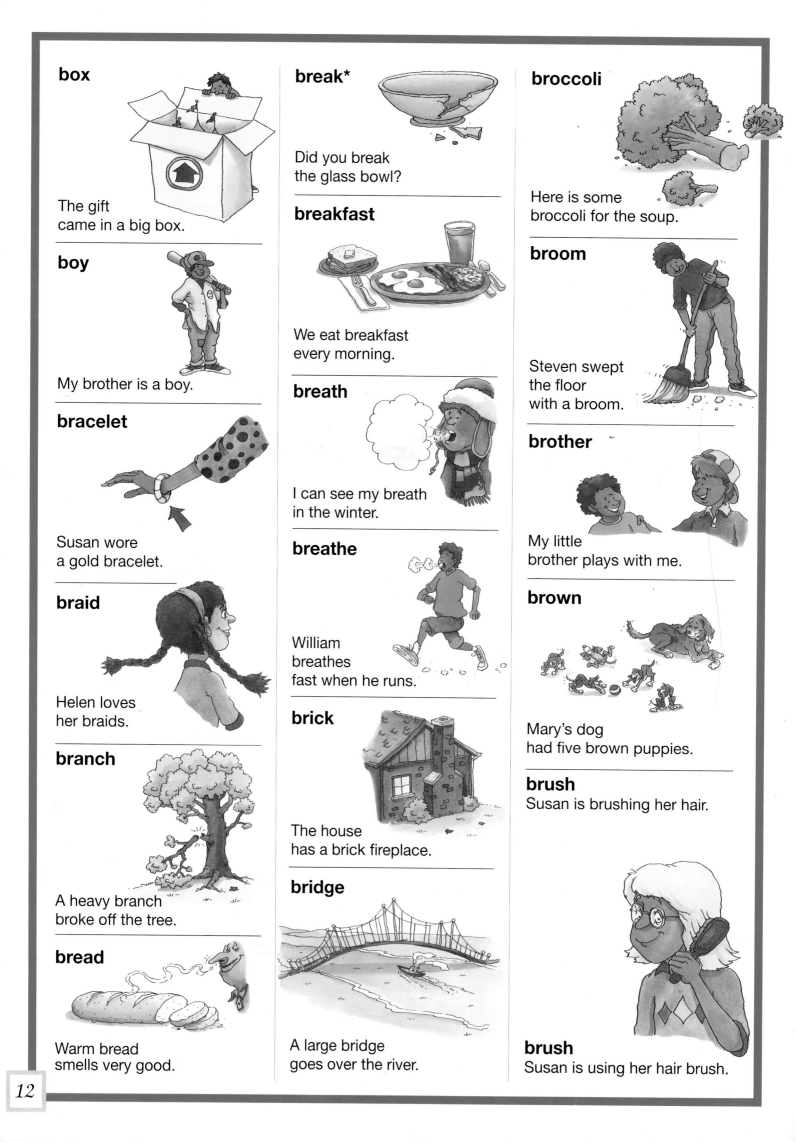

box

The gift came in a big box.

boy

My brother is a boy.

bracelet

Susan wore a gold bracelet.

braid

Helen loves her braids.

branch

A heavy branch broke off the tree.

bread

Warm bread smells very good.

break*

Did you break the glass bowl?

breakfast

We eat breakfast every morning.

breath

I can see my breath in the winter.

breathe

William breathes fast when he runs.

brick

The house has a brick fireplace.

bridge

A large bridge goes over the river.

broccoli

Here is some broccoli for the soup.

broom

Steven swept the floor with a broom.

brother

My little brother plays with me.

brown

Mary's dog had five brown puppies.

brush

Susan is brushing her hair.

brush

Susan is using her hair brush.

bubble

The bathtub
is full of bubbles.

bucket

Grandpa spilled
a bucket of water.

buckle

The belt has
a gold buckle.

buffalo

Buffalo are
big and strong.

build*

Dad will
build us a tree house.

building

The building near
the church is a school.

bull

The bull stood in the pasture.

bulletin board

Pictures hang
on the bulletin board.

bun

Mom buys hamburger
buns at the bakery.

burn*

Five candles
are burning.

bus

A bus took
my class to the museum.

bush

The bush has
new green leaves.

busy

The bee is very busy.

butter

Butter is good on bread.

butterfly

A butterfly flew
over our heads.

button

Steven's shirt
has red buttons.

buy*

I bought a
balloon at the zoo.

by

Our dog sits by the gate.

CcCcCcCc

cabbage

Rabbits love cabbage.

cage

Is the parrot happy in its cage?

cake

We ate chocolate cake.

calculator

Add the numbers on the calculator.

calendar

The calendar tells us the date.

calf*

A baby cow is called a calf.

call
Susan called Steven.

call
This telephone call is for Steven.

camel

Camels are found in the desert.

camp

At camp we have a fire each night.

can

I will buy a can of peaches.

canal

A small boat went through the canal.

candle

Mother is lighting the candle with a match.

candy

The children ate too much candy.

cane

My grandpa walks with a cane.

canoe

We went for a canoe ride.

cap

Robert always wears his baseball cap.

car

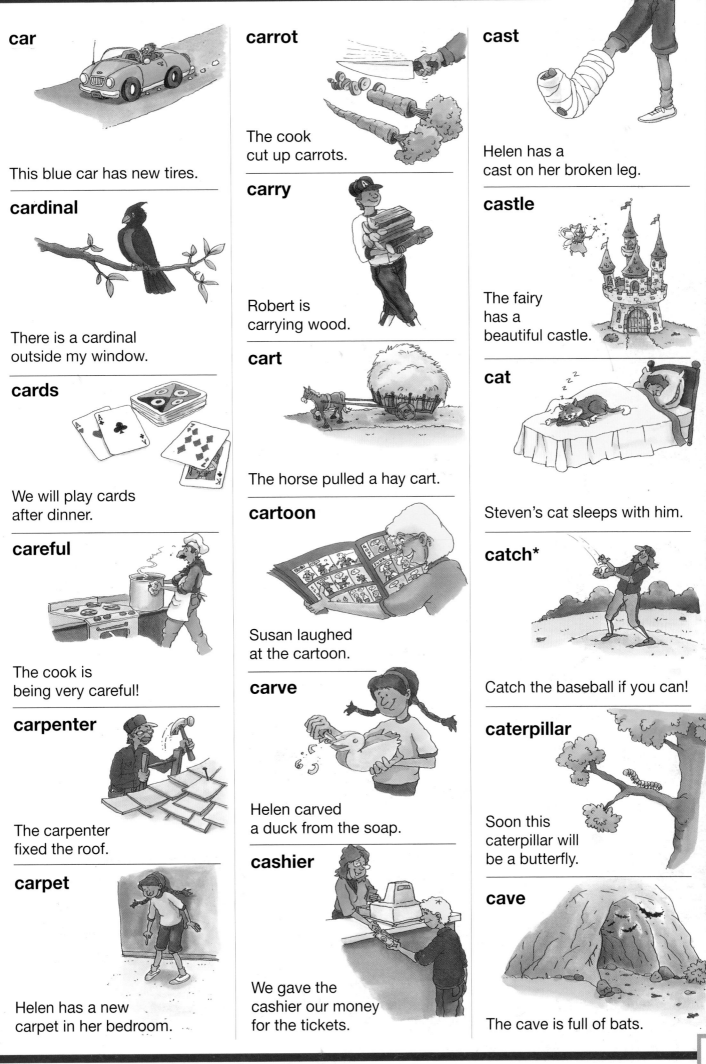

This blue car has new tires.

cardinal

There is a cardinal outside my window.

cards

We will play cards after dinner.

careful

The cook is being very careful!

carpenter

The carpenter fixed the roof.

carpet

Helen has a new carpet in her bedroom.

carrot

The cook cut up carrots.

carry

Robert is carrying wood.

cart

The horse pulled a hay cart.

cartoon

Susan laughed at the cartoon.

carve

Helen carved a duck from the soap.

cashier

We gave the cashier our money for the tickets.

cast

Helen has a cast on her broken leg.

castle

The fairy has a beautiful castle.

cat

Steven's cat sleeps with him.

catch*

Catch the baseball if you can!

caterpillar

Soon this caterpillar will be a butterfly.

cave

The cave is full of bats.

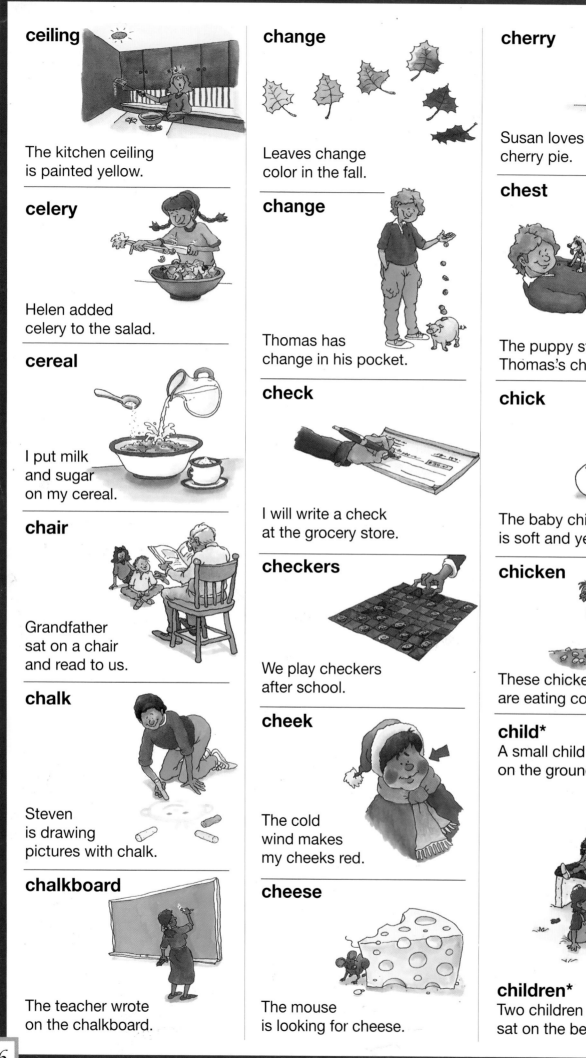

ceiling

The kitchen ceiling is painted yellow.

celery

Helen added celery to the salad.

cereal

I put milk and sugar on my cereal.

chair

Grandfather sat on a chair and read to us.

chalk

Steven is drawing pictures with chalk.

chalkboard

The teacher wrote on the chalkboard.

change

Leaves change color in the fall.

change

Thomas has change in his pocket.

check

I will write a check at the grocery store.

checkers

We play checkers after school.

cheek

The cold wind makes my cheeks red.

cheese

The mouse is looking for cheese.

cherry

Susan loves cherry pie.

chest

The puppy stood on Thomas's chest.

chick

The baby chick is soft and yellow.

chicken

These chickens are eating corn.

child*
A small child sat on the ground.

children*
Two children sat on the bench.

16

chimney

Smoke came out of the chimney.

chin

Helen has chocolate on her chin.

chipmunk

Chipmunks have striped backs.

chocolate

The bakery sells chocolate cookies.

church

I go to church with my grandma.

circle

Robert drew two circles on his paper.

circus

The circus has three acrobats.

city

The city has ten new buildings.

clap

The baby will clap hands with you.

clarinet

Mary plays the clarinet in the band.

class

I have a picture of my class at school.

classroom

Our classroom has many desks.

claw

A tiger has sharp claws.

clay

Steven made a clay rabbit.

clean
Dad cleans the windows with rags.

clean
The window is very clean.

clear

Glass is clear.

climb

Mary is climbing the ladder.

clock

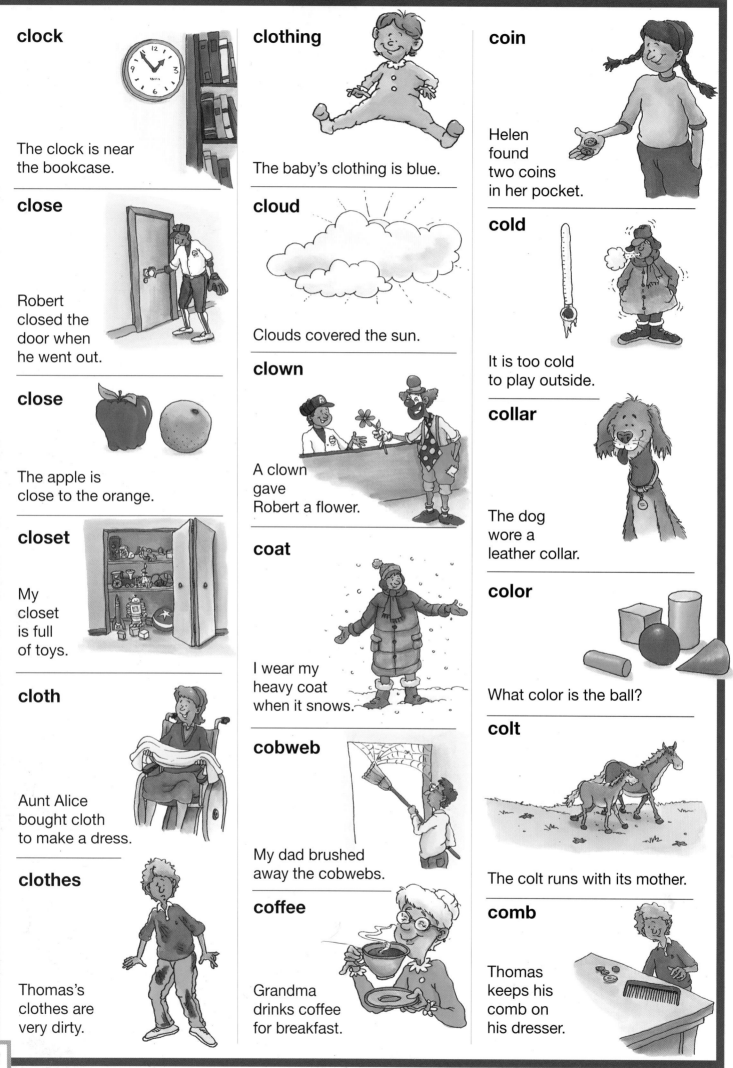

The clock is near the bookcase.

close

Robert closed the door when he went out.

close

The apple is close to the orange.

closet

My closet is full of toys.

cloth

Aunt Alice bought cloth to make a dress.

clothes

Thomas's clothes are very dirty.

clothing

The baby's clothing is blue.

cloud

Clouds covered the sun.

clown

A clown gave Robert a flower.

coat

I wear my heavy coat when it snows.

cobweb

My dad brushed away the cobwebs.

coffee

Grandma drinks coffee for breakfast.

coin

Helen found two coins in her pocket.

cold

It is too cold to play outside.

collar

The dog wore a leather collar.

color

What color is the ball?

colt

The colt runs with its mother.

comb

Thomas keeps his comb on his dresser.

come*

Come into
the house.

comet

Helen saw a
comet in the sky.

comfortable

This couch is
so very comfortable!

compass

Dad looked
at his compass.

completely

My plate is
completely clean!

computer

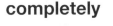

William is
playing games
on his computer.

cone

We ate ice cream cones.

contain

The large bottle
contains milk.

conversation

Robert and Susan
are having a conversation.

cook
The cook is
cooking vegetables
in a pot.

cook
The cook is wearing
a white apron.

cookie

Mom is baking
large chocolate cookies.

cool

Cool lemonade
is good in
the summer.

corn

Corn is growing in this field.

corner

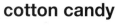

William waits at
the corner for the bus.

costume

Mary wore
a new costume.

cotton

Cotton
for our
clothes comes
from plants.

cotton candy

We ate pink
cotton candy at the circus.

couch

Dad is sleeping on the couch.

cough

Please cover
your mouth
when you cough!

cousin

My cousins
are my aunt's children.

cover

Grandpa
covers the
plants on
cold nights.

covers

Helen is
under the covers.

cow

The cows
sleep in the barn at night.

cowboy

The cowboy
put the saddle
on the horse.

coyote

Coyotes live
in the mountains.

cracker

Mary adds
crackers to her soup.

crane

A crane
lifted the car.

crane

This crane
is standing
in the water.

crate

What is in the crate?

crayon

Thomas
drew a
picture with crayons.

cream

My dad puts
cream in his coffee.

crocodile

We took a
picture of a crocodile.

crop

The crop
of tomatoes grew fast.

crosswalk

The
crosswalk
is painted
with white stripes.

crowd

A big crowd
was at the circus.

crown

The queen's crown has jewels on it.

crush

Dad crushed the can with his hand.

crust

The crust is the best part of a pie.

crutch

William walks with a crutch.

cry

The baby will cry if her bottle is empty.

cube

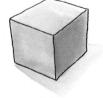

A cube has six sides.

cucumber

Cucumbers are a summer vegetable.

cup

Grandpa has a cup of tea after dinner.

cupboard

Dishes are kept in the cupboard.

curb

We stood near the curb to wait for the bus.

curly

William has curly black hair.

curtain

The curtains blew in the wind.

curve

The mountain road has many curves.

cut*

Robert cut the apple with a sharp knife.

cute

All babies are cute.

cymbal

Would you like to play the cymbals?

Dd *Dd* **Dd** *Dd*

dad

I call my father *dad*.

daisy

A vase of daisies is sitting on our table.

dance

Mary and William are dancing.

dance

Mary went to the dance with William.

dancer

The dancer wore red shoes.

dandelion

There are dandelions in our yard.

dark

It is dark outside.

date

Look at the calendar to find the date.

daughter

This woman has two daughters.

day

This is the day!

deck

The deck of the sailboat is painted white.

deep

Can you swim in the deep end of the pool?

deer*

Are there deer in the forest?

delicious

Apricots are delicious!

dent

There is a dent in this pan.

dentist

The dentist gave me a new toothbrush.

desert

In the desert it is very dry.

desk

The teacher sits at the desk.

dessert

We are having
ice cream for dessert.

dice*

Throw the dice
to play this game.

dictionary

How many pictures
are in your dictionary?

difficult

It is difficult
to walk on
your hands.

dig*

Thomas digs
in the sand
for treasure.

dim

The light from
the candle
was too dim.

dining room

Our dining room
has a table and six chairs.

dinner

We ate dinner
at a restaurant.

dinosaur

We saw dinosaurs
at the museum.

dirt

Do not sweep dirt
under the rug.

dirty

Please clean
your dirty shoes!

dish

My dad
washed the dishes.

dive*

Susan dived into the pool.

divide

A fence divides
our yard from your yard.

do*

What is
she doing?

dock

The passengers
waited on the dock.

doctor

The doctor
listens to
Robert's heart.

dog

What is my dog's name?

doll

Mary has
a doll with curly hair.

dollar

I put a dollar
in my bank.

dollhouse

The dollhouse
has tiny doors and windows.

dolphin

Dolphins swim in the ocean.

donkey

Robert rode
a donkey up the mountain.

door

Grandpa
opened the
door and looked outside.

doorbell

Mary rang
the doorbell.

doorman*

The
doorman
waits near the door.

dough

Robert made
dough for the bread.

down

Robert skied
down the hill.

dozen

There are a dozen
eggs in a box.

dragon

The dragon
lives in a cave.

draw*

Susan drew
a picture of her brother.

drawer

The drawer
is full of paper and pencils.

dream*
Mary dreamed
she was
in a palace.

dream
Mary's dream
made her happy.

dress
Helen is dressing for a party.

dress
Helen's party dress is pink.

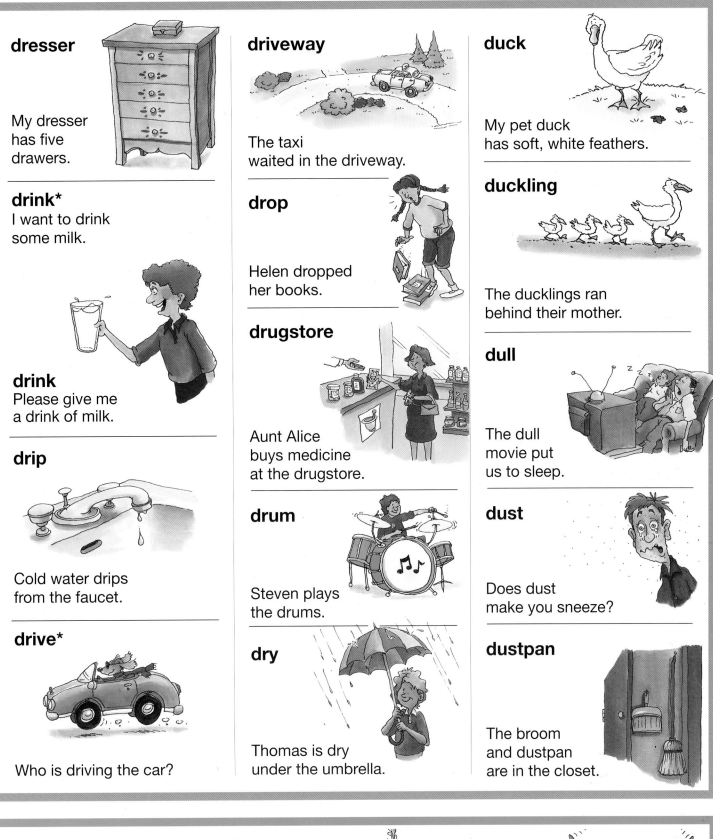

dresser

My dresser has five drawers.

drink*

I want to drink some milk.

drink

Please give me a drink of milk.

drip

Cold water drips from the faucet.

drive*

Who is driving the car?

driveway

The taxi waited in the driveway.

drop

Helen dropped her books.

drugstore

Aunt Alice buys medicine at the drugstore.

drum

Steven plays the drums.

dry

Thomas is dry under the umbrella.

duck

My pet duck has soft, white feathers.

duckling

The ducklings ran behind their mother.

dull

The dull movie put us to sleep.

dust

Does dust make you sneeze?

dustpan

The broom and dustpan are in the closet.

Ee*Ee*Ee*Ee*

each

Each flower is yellow.

eagle

The eagle flies to its nest.

ear

Helen washed
behind her ears.

early

William came
to school early.

earmuffs

Robert wore
earmuffs in the snowstorm.

earring

My mother
wears long,
silver earrings.

Earth

We live on the planet Earth.

easel

William's
picture sat on the easel.

easy

Floating on my back is easy!

eat*

We should eat
fruits and vegetables.

egg

Grandma will
cook two eggs.

elbow

Mary hit her
elbow on the table.

electricity

This lamp is
using electricity.

elephant

An elephant
walked in the circus parade.

elevator

The
elevator
carried us
to the top
of the building.

empty

One bottle is empty.

end

Where is the end of the rope?

engine

The mechanic
fixed the car's engine.

entrance

This gate is
the entrance to our yard.

envelope

Lick the envelope to close it.

equator

The equator goes around the Earth.

erase

Helen is erasing the blackboard.

eraser

Steven bought pencils with large erasers.

evening

The sun goes down in the evening.

every

Every child smiled.

exam

Mary is taking an exam.

eye

My eyes are blue.

eyebrow

Our eyebrows are above our eyes.

F f F f F f F f

face

Please put a smile on your face!

factory

This factory makes cars.

fairy

The fairy gave the queen some jewels.

fall*

Jimmy falls down.

fall

My family rakes leaves in the fall.

family

This is a picture of my family.

fan

Helen sits near the fan when she is hot.

far

The sun is far from the Earth.

farm

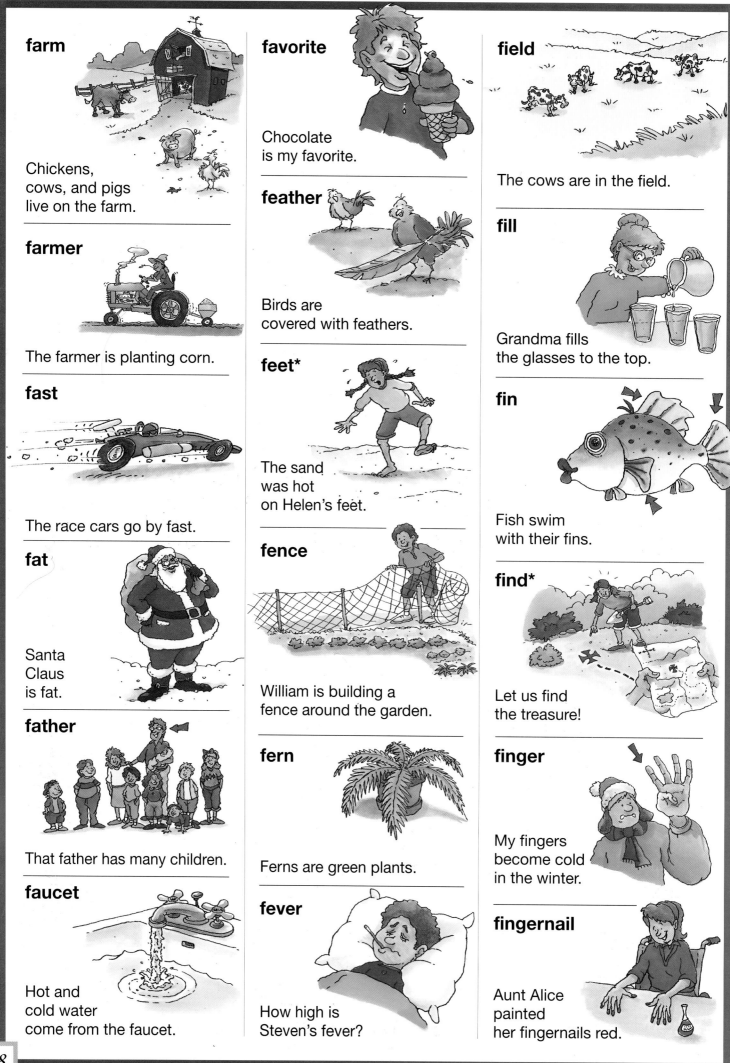

Chickens, cows, and pigs live on the farm.

farmer

The farmer is planting corn.

fast

The race cars go by fast.

fat

Santa Claus is fat.

father

That father has many children.

faucet

Hot and cold water come from the faucet.

favorite

Chocolate is my favorite.

feather

Birds are covered with feathers.

feet*

The sand was hot on Helen's feet.

fence

William is building a fence around the garden.

fern

Ferns are green plants.

fever

How high is Steven's fever?

field

The cows are in the field.

fill

Grandma fills the glasses to the top.

fin

Fish swim with their fins.

find*

Let us find the treasure!

finger

My fingers become cold in the winter.

fingernail

Aunt Alice painted her fingernails red.

28

fire

Uncle Edward lit the fire with a match.

fire engine

The fire engine raced to the fire.

fire fighter

A fire fighter wears a hat, a raincoat, and boots.

fireplace

This house has a fireplace in the living room.

first

Thomas is first in line.

fish*
Grandpa wants fish for dinner.

fish
Grandpa is fishing at the lake.

fisherman*

The fisherman caught two fish.

fix

Helen will fix the broken toy.

flag

Helen carried the flag in the parade.

flame

The candle flame is yellow.

flamingo

A flamingo has long legs.

flashlight

Mary carried a flashlight to see in the dark.

flat

Paper is flat.

flavor

What flavor of ice cream do you like?

float

The little girl's balloons floated away.

floor

The bedroom floor is covered with clothes.

florist

The florist sells flowers and plants.

flour

The cook adds flour to the dough.

29

flower

Are these flowers orange?

flowerbed

The gardener watered the flowerbed.

flu

Robert is in bed with the flu.

flute

Steven plays the flute in the orchestra.

fly*

The airplane is flying over the town.

fly

A fly flies around the food.

fog

Gray fog covers the city.

follow

The cat followed me home.

food

The food is on the table.

foolish

Playing with matches is foolish.

foot*

The baby played with its foot.

football

Robert plays football.

footprint

Our footprints show in the wet sand.

footstool

The little girl sat on a footstool.

for

We are having turkey for dinner.

forehead

My forehead is above my eyebrows.

forest

The forest is full of trees.

forget*

Susan always forgets her glasses.

fork

Mary ate her salad with a fork.

fountain

There is a fountain in the park.

fox

The fox ran through the yard.

freckles

Robert has freckles on his nose.

freeze*

Water freezes into ice in the winter.

freezer

Our freezer has ice cream in it.

french fries

Steven ate french fries with his hamburger.

friend

My friend likes to play ball.

frog

A frog jumped into the pond.

from

Juice comes from fruit.

frost

We saw frost on the lawn this morning.

fruit

Helen had some fruit for a snack.

full

Helen's plate is full of food.

fun

Birthday parties are so much fun!

funnel

Dad put the oil in the car with a funnel.

fur

The wolf has heavy fur.

furnace

The furnace makes our house warm.

furniture

Grandpa's old furniture is in the attic.

GgGgGgGg

game

Mary and
her sister play
games after school.

garage

We keep
our car in the garage.

garden

Thomas planted
flowers in his garden.

gardener

A gardener
must pull weeds.

garden hose

Thomas
waters the plants
with the garden hose.

gas

Our stove uses gas.

gasoline

The lawn mower
runs on gasoline.

gate

William
opened
the gate
in the fence.

ghost

There is no
such thing as a ghost.

gift

I took a gift
to the birthday party.

gills

Gills help fish
breathe in the water.

giraffe

The giraffe
is a very
tall animal.

girl

My sister is a girl.

give*

Give the
box to your brother.

glad

We are glad
you came for dinner.

glass

Grandfather
filled the
glass with milk.

glass

The
window is made of glass.

glasses

William wears glasses to help him see.

globe

A globe sits on the teacher's desk.

glove

Gloves keep our hands warm in the winter.

glue
Who glued the cup together?

glue
Who spilled glue on the table?

go*

We will go to school.

goat

Goats eat many things!

goggles

Helen wears goggles under the water.

gold

The man has a gold watch.

good*

The weather is good for playing in the park.

goose*

Susan has a pet goose.

gorilla

The gorilla at the zoo eats fruits and vegetables.

gosling

A gosling is a baby goose.

grandfather

My grandfather is my dad's father.

grandmother

My grandmother is my dad's mother.

grandpa

Grandpa reads a book to me.

grandparent

Grandparents are the parents of your parents.

grape

Grapes are green or purple.

grapefruit

Thomas ate grapefruit for lunch.

grass

The grass
in the yard is too tall.

grasshopper

Grasshoppers have wings.

gravy

Mary put gravy
on her potatoes.

gray

Thomas's parrot is gray.

green

Green is
the color of grass.

greenhouse

A greenhouse
is a glass
house for plants.

grocery store

GROCERY STORE

Grandpa bought a fish
at the grocery store.

ground

Steven sat
on the ground and thought.

group

A group of
children sat in a circle.

grow*

Jimmy is
growing fast.

guest

Our guest
rang the
doorbell.

guitar

William
plays the guitar.

Hh*Hh*Hh*Hh*

hair

William is
brushing his hair.

half*

Mary ate half the melon.

ham

We had ham for dinner.

hamburger

I had a hamburger for dinner.

hammer
Thomas hammered
the nail into
the wood.

hammer
Thomas hit
the nail with a hammer.

hammock

Robert sleeps in a hammock.

hand

Steven washed his hands.

handkerchief*

Thomas always carries a handkerchief.

handsome

The actor was very handsome.

hang*

Mary hangs her coat behind the door.

hanger

The closet is full of empty hangers.

happy

People smile when they are happy.

hard

It is hard to walk on your hands.

hard

The floor is hard!

harp

A harp has many strings.

hat

My aunt always wears a hat to church.

have*

They have red hats.

hay

Horses and cows eat hay.

head

The parrot sat on my head!

healthy

Steven and Helen look very healthy.

heart

My heart is right here.

heat

Too much heat will burn the carrots.

heavy

The box is
too heavy to lift.

helicopter

A helicopter
flew over our house.

help

Aunt Alice
helps Jimmy
stand up.

hen

The hen watched her chicks.

herd

A herd of sheep
walked on the road.

here

Put it here, please.

high

The cookies are on
the high shelf.

hill

The puppy
ran up the hill.

hippopotamus

A hippopotamus
walked in the river.

hit*

Robert hit
the baseball with the bat.

hockey

Hockey is
played on ice skates.

hoe

Mary
hoed her
garden often.

hoe

Thomas used his
hoe to weed his garden.

hold*

I can hold
the kitten in my hand.

hole

The dog
is digging
a hole
for its bone.

home

Home is
where you
hang your hat.

homework

Steven has no
more homework to do!

honey

Bears love honey.

hood

Helen's winter coat has a hood.

hoof*

The horse's hoof has a new shoe.

hoop

The circus dog jumped through the hoop.

horn

Some animals have horns.

horse

Thomas rides horses at the ranch.

hose

Susan used the hose to water the garden.

hospital

My uncle is in the hospital.

hot

It is hot in the summer.

hotel

We slept in a hotel for a night.

hour

Mary did her homework in an hour.

house

Steven lives in a house on a corner.

how

How hot is it?

hug

My mom hugs me when she is happy.

hump

Camels have humps on their backs.

hungry

The dog is very hungry.

hunt

Helen is hunting for her shoes.

hurt*
Helen ran into the door and hurt her head.

I i *I i* I i *I i*

I i

ice

In cold weather, water freezes into ice.

ice cream

Ice cream melts fast in the summer.

ice skate

These new ice skates are for Robert's birthday.

icicle

Icicles hang from the roof in winter.

in front of

The mailbox is in front of the house.

ink

Thomas's pen uses black ink.

insect

Grasshoppers and flies are insects.

into

Put the banana into the lunch bag.

iron

Careful — the iron is hot!

island

An island is surrounded by water.

J j *J j* J j *J j*

J j

jacket

Robert wears a jacket in the spring.

jam

Mary loves toast with jam.

jeans

Robert wears old jeans to clean the floor.

Jeep

The Jeep drove up the mountain road.

jelly

Some cakes have jelly in them.

jet

Have you flown on a jet?

jewel

Her necklace has many jewels on it.

jeweler

The jeweler sells rings and bracelets.

jigsaw puzzle

Robert put together a jigsaw puzzle.

jog

Steven and his dad jog in the park.

juggle

How many balls is the clown juggling?

juice

Jimmy wants juice.

jump

Mary can jump over the fence.

jungle

It is very hot in the jungle.

jungle gym

The children climb on the jungle gym.

KkKkKkKk

Kk

kangaroo

A kangaroo can jump very far.

keep*

Steven's mom keeps all his exams.

ketchup

Helen put ketchup on her hamburger.

kettle

The cook is stirring a kettle of soup.

key

The door can be opened with this key.

kick

Robert gave the ball a hard kick.

kick

Robert kicked the football.

kid

A kid is a baby goat.

king

The king lives in a castle.

kitchen

We eat in the kitchen.

kite

Thomas's kite is high in the sky.

kitten

My cat is a good mother to her kittens.

knee

Steven hurt his knee playing football.

knife*

Mary dropped her knife on the floor.

knit*

Grandma knit her dog a sweater.

knot

Susan tied her shoelaces in knots.

Ll Ll Ll Ll

label

Robert read the label on the soup can.

lace

Our curtains are made of lace.

ladder

The fire fighter climbed a ladder to the roof.

lake

We like to fish and swim at the lake.

lamb

The lambs love to play.

lamp

A large lamp
lights up the bedroom.

lap

When I sit
down, my cat
jumps up on my lap.

large

The jacket is
too large for Mary.

last

Who wants
the last piece of cake?

late

Mom was
late for work.

laugh

Susan is laughing at
the clown.

laugh

Susan's laugh
is very loud.

laundry

This pile of
laundry has to be washed.

lawn

Thomas sat
on the lawn
under a tree.

**lawn
mower**

Dad cut the grass
with the lawn mower.

lazy

Mary was lazy
and would not
clean her room.

leaf*

A leaf fell off the
tree and into my lap.

leap*

It's fun to
leap over
puddles in the rain.

learn

Aa Bb Cc Dd Ff
Dog
Cat M

At school we
are learning to read.

leather

Robert's shoes are leather.

leave*

I leave the
house for school
after breakfast.

left

William held
the balloon
in his left hand.

41

leg

The spider has very long legs.

lemon

Helen is squeezing lemons.

lemonade

We drink lemonade when the weather is hot.

leopard

A leopard lives at the zoo.

less*

Robert has less dessert than Susan does.

lesson

It is time for Helen's violin lesson.

letter

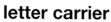

Will you write me a letter?

letter carrier

The letter carrier fills our mailbox.

lettuce

William put lettuce in the salad.

librarian

The librarian helps me find books.

lick

Mary is licking her ice cream cone.

lift

Please lift the top of the box.

light*

Mother is lighting a candle.

lightbulb

Mary put a new lightbulb in the lamp.

lightning

Lightning lights up the night sky.

like

One is like the other.

like

Steven likes ice cream!

lime

What color is the lime?

line

I do not like standing in line.

lion

The lions are sleeping.

lip

Helen bit her lip.

list

Shopping list
Milk
Eggs
Flour
Pop
Napkins
Sugar
Cheese

How many
things are on the list?

listen

The students
listen to the music.

little

The baby's shoes are little.

live

The dog
lives in a small house.

living room

Our living room
has a fireplace.

lizard

A lizard sat
on a rock in the sun.

lobster

The fisherman
caught a lobster.

lock

Helen locked the
door when
she left.

lock

There are two
locks on the door.

log

Uncle
Edward
carried in
some logs.

lollipop

Jimmy
dropped
his lollipop.

long

The pants
are too long
for Thomas.

look

Helen is looking
at the cherry pie.

loud

The bell
is very loud!

love

Mommy loves
Jimmy very much.

lunch

We ate soup
and sandwiches for lunch.

43

MmMm MmMm

magazine

Thomas reads magazines at home.

magician

The magician pulled a rabbit out of his hat.

magnet

The nails are pulled by a magnet.

mail

A letter came for Susan in the mail.

mailbox

Every home has a mailbox.

make*

Helen made a pie for dessert.

make-believe

Children play make-believe.

man*

My uncle is a tall man.

mane

The horse has a long mane.

many

There are many candles on the cake!

map

Robert has a map of the United States.

mask

The costume has a silly mask.

match

Dad lit the fire with matches.

match

These socks do not match.

meal

Breakfast is the morning meal.

meat

Dad cut up the meat for sandwiches.

44

mechanic

A mechanic fixes cars at the gas station.

medal

The runner won a medal.

medicine

Robert's mother gave him some medicine.

medium

Medium is between large and small.

melon

Grandfather planted melons in his garden.

melt

Helen's ice cream melted.

menu

I read the menu at the restaurant.

mess

Thomas's face is a mess.

microphone

The singer sang into a microphone.

microscope

The microscope makes small things look big.

milk

Milk gives you strong bones and teeth.

mirror

Helen is looking at herself in the mirror.

mittens

Robert wears his mittens outside in the snow.

mix

William mixed flour into the cookie dough.

mom

I call my mother *mom*.

money

Robert bought a ball with his money.

monkey

The monkey jumped from branch to branch.

month

There are four
weeks in a month.

moon

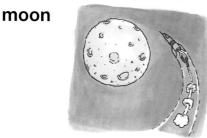

The astronauts
went to the moon.

more*

Jimmy wants more milk.

morning

We have
breakfast every morning.

mosquito

A mosquito bit me!

moth

The moth looks
like a butterfly.

mother

My mother reads to me.

mountain

The mountains
are covered with snow.

mouse*

The mouse ran
into a hole in the wall.

mouth

I opened my
mouth for the dentist.

movie

The children
watched a movie.

much

There is much food here!

mud

Pigs love to roll in the mud.

museum

A museum
contains many statues.

mushroom

We found
mushrooms in the wet grass.

music

Helen wrote
new music for
the band to play.

mustache

Robert's uncle
has a large,
brown mustache.

mustard

Mustard
is good
on ham
sandwiches.

NnNnNnNn

nail
Robert nailed the sign to the fence.

nail
Robert used four nails.

name
Whose name is *Jimmy*?

nap
Grandpa is taking a nap.

nap
He is napping on the sofa.

napkin
Mary dropped her napkin.

narrow
The mailbox is too narrow.

near
The lamp is near the chair.

neck
Giraffes have long necks.

necklace
Helen is wearing a gold necklace.

necktie
Robert is wearing a necktie.

need
We need more milk.

needle
Grandma sews with a needle.

nest
The baby birds are waiting in the nest.

net
I hit the volleyball over the net.

never
The teacher is never late!

new
Steven needs new shoes.

newspaper

Helen is reading
the newspaper.

night

Nights are quiet
in the mountains.

noise

The parrot
is making too much noise.

noodles

My aunt
cooked noodles for lunch.

noon

William is
hungry by noon.

nose

In the
winter my
nose becomes red.

note

William will
make a note
of the address.

notebook

He is writing the
address in his notebook.

notepad

There is a notepad
near the telephone.

number

There are
numbers in my address.

nurse

A nurse helps
make patients healthy.

nuts

Mary's
ice cream
has nuts on top.

OoOoOoOo

Oo

oar

The oars are in the rowboat.

ocean

Whales live in the ocean.

octopus

An octopus has eight arms.

off

Steven fell off his horse.

office

My dad goes
to an office to work.

often

The traffic light changes often.

oil

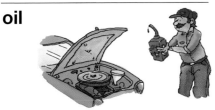

Cars have to have oil and gasoline.

old

Mary wore a new shirt and her old jeans.

omelet

I cooked an omelet with eggs and cheese.

on

Robert is on the bicycle.

onion

My dad eats onions on his hamburger.

open

The baby opened her mouth to cry.

open

The rain came in the open window.

orange

Mix red and yellow to make orange.

orange

Robert ate an orange for lunch.

orchestra

The orchestra played for more than an hour!

ostrich

The ostrich is a very large bird.

other

The other piece of cake is yours!

out

Steven went out the door.

outside

The outside of the box is gold.

oven

The cook baked a pie in the oven.

over

The airplane flew over our house.

owl

Owls hunt for food at night.

PpPpPpPp

package

There was a package for me in the mailbox.

page

Jimmy drew on this page.

pail

Jimmy took his pail to the beach.

pain

Robert had a pain in his head.

paint
Helen painted a picture of her cat.

paint
The red paint dripped on the rug.

paintbrush

Steven put the paintbrush into the paint.

pajamas

Mary wears pajamas with feet.

palace

The king and queen live in a palace.

pan

Mother cooks eggs in a pan.

panda

The zoo has a new panda.

pants

Robert wore a white shirt and black pants.

paper

Helen's paper is on the bulletin board.

parachute

The man jumped from the airplane with a parachute.

parade

There were clowns in the parade.

paramedic

Paramedics help people who are hurt.

parents

My parents are Mommy and Daddy.

park

Our park has grass, flowers, and benches.

parrot

Aunt Alice's
parrot talks to her.

part

The boy ate part of the apple.

party

Jimmy is
having a birthday party.

passenger

Passengers
buy tickets to
ride the train.

paste
Someone left
the paste on
the table.

paste
Thomas pasted
his picture on the page.

pasture

The cows
are in the pasture.

path

William followed
a path in the forest.

patient

A nurse
gives the patient medicine.

paw

The dog
held up
its paw.

pea

I like peas
and carrots.

peach

Robert ate
a peach with his cereal.

peanut

Helen
eats peanuts
at the movies.

pear

Here are two
pears and an apple.

pebble

Susan
dropped
a pebble
into the water.

pen

The student
wrote with a pen.

pencil

William
draws
pictures with a pencil.

pencil sharpener

There is
a pencil
sharpener
in the classroom.

51

penguin

Penguins live on the ice.

people

Some people came to our house.

pepper

Pepper is black, and salt is white.

person

One person was late for school.

pet
The puppy is Susan's pet.

pet
Susan is petting her puppy.

petal

This flower has soft, red petals.

pharmacist

Aunt Alice buys pills from the pharmacist.

pharmacy

The pharmacy sells medicine.

phone booth

Dad is calling home from a phone booth.

photograph

Mary is holding a photograph of her dad.

piano

Robert plays the piano while his sister sings.

picnic

We ate chicken at our picnic.

picture

In a museum, pictures hang on the walls.

pie

Who ate a piece of pie?

piece

That is a very large piece!

pig

There are many pigs on Uncle Edward's farm.

piggy bank

Mary keeps money in her piggy bank.

pile

A pile of dirt
covered the sidewalk.

pill

The nurse
gave Thomas a yellow pill.

pillow

My bed has soft
pillows for my head.

pilot

The pilot
is flying the airplane.

pin

Pins are very sharp!

pineapple

Susan put
pineapple
in the fruit salad.

pink

Susan
wore a
pink hat
and coat.

pitcher

Mary is the
pitcher on her
baseball team.

pitcher

Thomas
spilled the
milk pitcher.

place

A bed is a place for sleeping.

plain

The gift
came in
plain paper
with no ribbons.

plain

Wheat grows on the plains.

planet

The planets circle the sun.

plant

The farmer
is planting corn.

plant

The window is full of plants.

plate

William has
meat and
potatoes on his plate.

play

Mary plays
the guitar.

play

The children
are playing
on the swings.

playground

Robert goes to the playground after school.

please

More cake, please.

plumber

A plumber came to fix the sink.

pocket

What is in your pocket?

point

Susan is pointing at the cat.

point

The needle has a sharp point.

polar bear

Polar bears have white fur.

police

The police keep us safe.

police car

A police car raced down the street.

policeman*

A policeman gave my dad a ticket.

policewoman*

The policewoman showed me the way.

pond

Frogs and fish live in the pond.

ponytail

Mary tied a ribbon around her ponytail.

pool

We swim and play in a pool.

popcorn

Steven buys popcorn at the movies.

porch

I love to sit on the porch at sunset.

porthole

A porthole is a window on a boat.

post office

Helen buys stamps at the post office.

54

pot

Susan is stirring the pot of soup.

potato

Grandma cut up potatoes to make french fries.

potato chips

Robert ate potato chips at the picnic.

powder

Mary powdered the baby.

practice

Helen is practicing the violin.

present

These birthday presents are for Jimmy.

pretty

The garden is filled with pretty flowers.

price

The prices for the food are on the menu.

prince

A prince is the son of a king and queen.

princess

The princess wore a small crown.

prize

Robert won a prize for running fast.

puddle

The children walked through the puddles.

pull

Mary pulled the wagon down the sidewalk.

pumpkin

Mommy carved a face in my pumpkin.

puppet

William has a puppet on his hand.

puppy

I love my new puppy!

purple

Grape juice is purple.

purse

Susan carries her purse on her shoulder.

55

push

Steven pushed
his plate away.

put*

Steven put his
hand on his head.

puzzle

This puzzle
is too hard.

QqQqQqQq

Qq

queen

The queen
wears jewels
and a crown.

quiet

SSSSHHHH

Please be quiet.

RrRrRrRr

Rr

radio

Helen's
radio is too loud.

raincoat

Susan has
a yellow raincoat.

rag

Thomas
cleaned up
the mess
with a rag.

rake

William rakes
the leaves with a rake.

rabbit

Thomas's
pet is a
white rabbit.

race
I will race you
to the tree.

rain

Rain came
from the
dark clouds.

rainbow

There was
a rainbow in the sky.

ranch

DUDE RANCH

Cowboys
live on ranches.

raspberries

Mary ate
raspberries
with her
ice cream.

race
Who will
win this race?

rat

The cat ran after the rat.

read*

William is reading Jimmy a story.

receive

Mary received a gift from William.

red

Apples, cherries, and raspberries are red.

refrigerator

Milk is kept in the refrigerator.

reins

William steers his horse by pulling the reins.

relative

My aunt and uncle are two of my relatives.

reporter

That reporter writes for a newspaper.

reptile

Snakes and alligators are reptiles.

restaurant

Steven and his dad ate dinner at a restaurant.

rhinoceros

The rhinoceros is a large animal with a horn.

ribbon

Susan's mother tied a ribbon in her hair.

rice

Helen likes chicken with rice.

ride*

William rides his bicycle to school.

right

Mary put her right hand on her heart.

right

Which is the right way?

ring*

William is ringing the dinner bell.

ring

Mom wears a wedding ring.

river

Do you see
the river in the valley?

road

That road goes
into the forest.

roar

The lion roared for food.

roast

Helen roasted
a turkey in the oven.

roast

The roast
cooked for hours!

robe

Robert wears
a robe over
his pajamas.

robin

Robins'
eggs are blue.

rock

Mary
found a
pretty rock
on the beach.

rock

Uncle Edward
loves to sit and rock.

roll

My dog can
roll over and sit up.

roller skates

Helen goes
fast on her
roller skates.

roof

Our house has a red roof.

room

Steven has his own room.

rooster

The rooster is
standing on the fence.

rope

William tied a
rope to his wagon.

rose

Roses smell so good!

round

The ball is round.

rowboat

The fisherman is sitting
in a rowboat on the lake.

rub

Thomas rubs his face with a towel.

rug

The cat is napping on the rug.

ruler

Thomas draws the line with a ruler.

run*

Helen runs faster than Susan.

runner

The runners are going very fast.

Ss Ss Ss Ss

sack

Steven carries his lunch in a sack.

sad

The little boy is sad.

saddle

Helen sat in the saddle on the horse.

safe

We are safe when our seat belts are fastened.

safe

Uncle Edward keeps his money in a safe.

sail

A small boat sailed on the lake.

sailboat

A sailboat is tied to the dock.

sailor

Sailors wear clean uniforms.

salad

Steven ate a salad with his dinner.

salt

William added salt to the popcorn.

sand

We built a castle from sand.

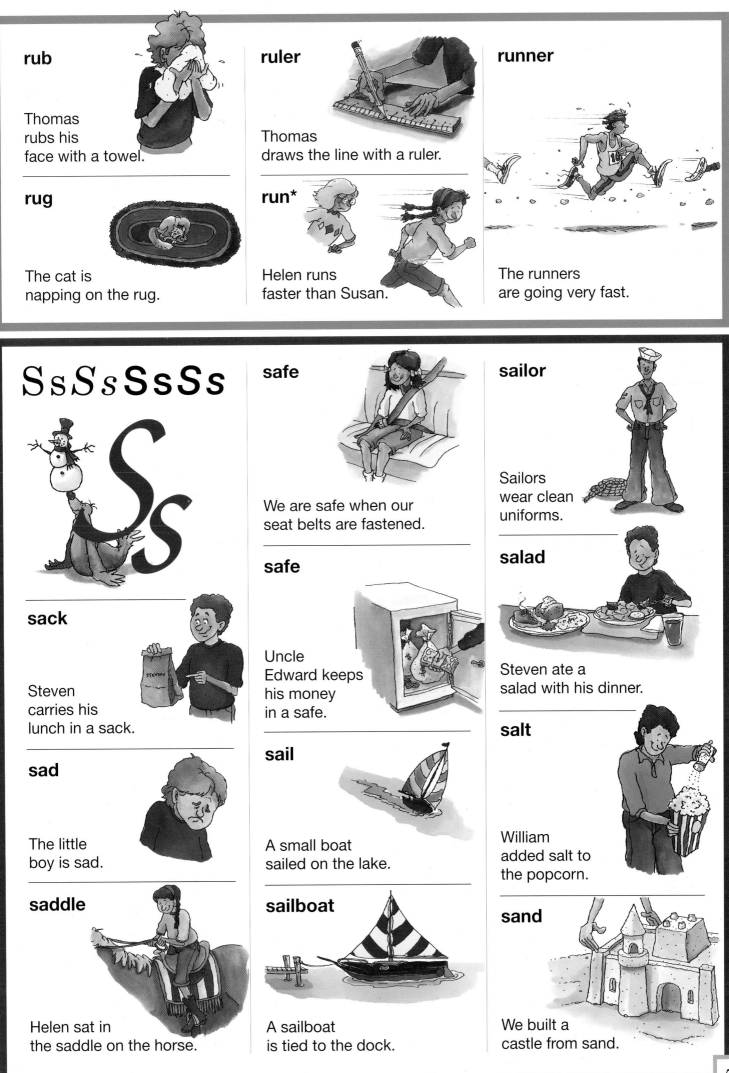

sandals

Susan wears sandals in the summer.

sandbox

William is playing in the sandbox.

sandwich

Robert's sandwich has ham and cheese in it.

Santa Claus

Does Santa Claus have a present for you?

saucer

Some tea spilled into the saucer.

sausage

Mary ate sausage and eggs for breakfast.

saw

Dad sawed logs for the fire.

saxophone

Mary is learning to play the saxophone.

scale

My pet fish is covered with gold scales.

scale

The heavy man stood on the scale.

scarecrow

The scarecrow keeps the birds away.

scarf*

Mary wore a pink scarf around her neck.

school

The school is a red-brick building.

school bus

The school bus is big and yellow.

scientist

The scientist is using his microscope.

scissors

Susan cut paper dolls with the scissors.

screw
Screws hold things together.

screwdriver
Dad is using the screwdriver.

sea

Whales and sharks swim in the sea.

seal

The seal can catch a basketball on its nose.

seashell

Thomas found some seashells at the beach.

seat

Thomas sat in a seat near the door.

seat belt

Wear your seat belt in the airplane.

seaweed

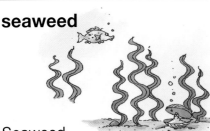

Seaweed grows in the ocean.

secretary

The secretary has a computer at her desk.

see*

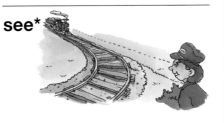

I can see the train coming.

seed

The bird is eating seeds.

seesaw

The seesaw goes up and down.

sell*

Steven sells ice cream in the park.

sew*

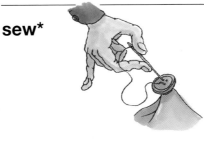

Will you sew this button on?

sewing machine

Mom makes clothes on the sewing machine.

shadow

The cat is playing with its shadow.

shark

A shark has a fin on its back.

sharp

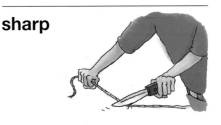

Steven cut the string with a sharp knife.

sheep*

The sheep ran away from the dog.

sheet

Helen's bed has clean sheets on it.

shelf*

The cereal is on the bottom shelf.

ship

This ship sails on the ocean.

shipwreck

There is an old shipwreck on the beach.

shirt

Mary wears her team's baseball shirt.

shoe

Whose red shoes are these?

shoelace

Thomas's shoes have black shoelaces.

shop

William is in a toy shop.

shop

He is shopping for a gift.

shore

We sat on the shore and watched the boats.

short

Steven is short, but Susan is tall.

shorts

Helen wears shorts to play ball.

shoulder

The parrot sat on Susan's shoulder.

shovel

The farmer is digging with a shovel.

show*

Steven is showing us his watch.

show*

The sun is showing a little bit.

shower

Thomas is in the shower.

sick

William is very sick.

side

Thomas has a pain in the side.

sidewalk

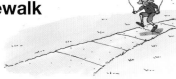

The little girl is jumping rope on the sidewalk.

sign

There is a sign in the yard of this house.

signature

Mary wrote her signature on the paper.

silly

We laugh when Grandpa wears a silly hat.

silver

William has a silver ring.

sing*
Mary is singing for her class.

singer
She is a very loud singer.

sink

Helen washed the dishes in the sink.

sister

I hold my little sister on my lap.

sit*

Jimmy sits up straight in the chair.

size

Is this shirt the right size?

skate

Thomas has some new skates.

skate

He is skating on the pond.

skateboard

William is riding his skateboard.

ski

Mom put our skis on the car top.

ski

We are all going skiing.

skirt

My skirt has flowers on it.

skunk

The skunk has a terrible smell.

sky

The sky is full of white clouds.

skyscraper

A skyscraper is a very tall building.

sled

Mary is riding her sled down the hill.

sleep*

Shhh, the baby is sleeping.

sleeve

I have a hole in my sleeve.

slide*

The children are sliding on the ice.

slow

Turtles are slow, and rabbits are fast.

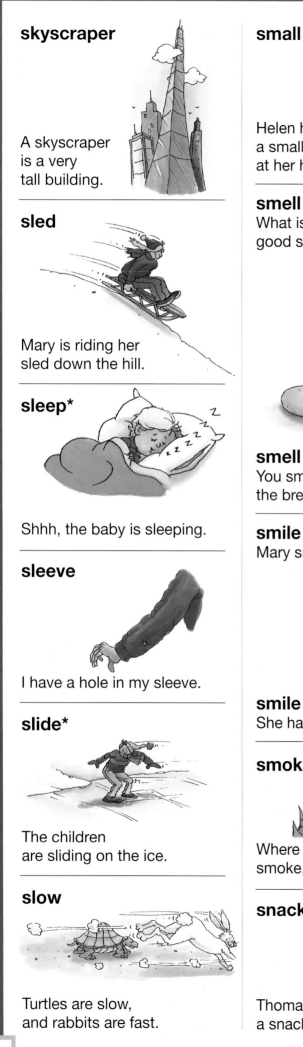

small

Helen has a small puppy at her house.

smell
What is that good smell?

smell
You smell the bread baking.

smile
Mary smiled at me.

smile
She has a pretty smile.

smoke

Where there is smoke, there is fire.

snack

Thomas ate a snack after school.

snail

The snail is very slow.

snake

Snakes are clean, dry reptiles.

sneeze

AAAHHCCHHOOOO!

Flowers make Mary sneeze.

snow

William is cleaning the snow off the sidewalk.

snowball

Helen threw a snowball at her brother.

snowflake

Many snowflakes fall in a snowstorm.

snowman*

The children built a snowman in the yard.

snowstorm

There was a snowstorm last night.

soap

Mary rubs the soap on her hands.

socks

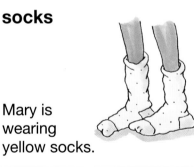

Mary is wearing yellow socks.

sofa

We sat on the sofa near the fireplace.

soft

A cat's fur is soft.

soft drink

Robert put ice in his soft drink.

some

Some blossoms are open.

somersault

Helen can do a somersault.

son

That woman has a son.

soon

I must go to bed soon.

soup

Steven ate tomato soup and crackers.

space

There is space for more books.

spaceship

This spaceship is on the moon.

sparrow

There are two sparrows in the tree.

speak*

Robert is speaking to Helen.

spider

There was a large, black spider on the wall.

spiderweb

There is a spiderweb in the corner.

spill

Who spilled the milk?

spin*

The top is spinning very fast.

spinach

Helen planted spinach in the garden.

spoke

Some spokes are broken.

sponge

Thomas wiped the table with a sponge.

spoon

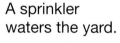

Grandfather stirs his coffee with a spoon.

sports

Robert loves sports.

spot

My dog is white with black spots.

spotlight

The singer stands in the spotlight.

spread*

Mary spread butter on the bread.

spring

Flowers come out in the spring.

sprinkler

A sprinkler waters the yard.

square

How many squares are there?

squeeze

Robert squeezed the ketchup bottle.

squirrel

A squirrel ran up the tree.

stable

The horses sleep in the stable.

stage

The band sits on the stage.

stairs

Helen walked up the stairs to her bedroom.

stamp

Mary was angry and stamped her foot.

stamp

The stamp goes on the envelope.

stand*

Please stand up straight!

stapler

The stapler is empty.

staples

Mary is putting staples in the stapler.

star

We see the stars at night.

starfish*

Helen found a starfish on the beach.

statue

The statue has no head.

steak

My dad cooks steak with mushrooms.

steer

Mary steered the bicycle around the hole.

stem

The flowers have very long stems.

step

Jimmy went up two steps.

stereo

William listens to the stereo.

stethoscope

The doctor listens to my heart with a stethoscope.

stick

Helen threw a stick for her dog to catch.

stilts

The man on stilts is as tall as the roof.

stir

Aunt Alice is stirring the gravy.

67

stirrups

Slide your feet into the stirrups.

stone

The wall was made of stones.

stop

We stopped the car for the red light.

stop sign

There is a stop sign at the corner.

storm

Rain, lightning, and wind came with the storm.

stove

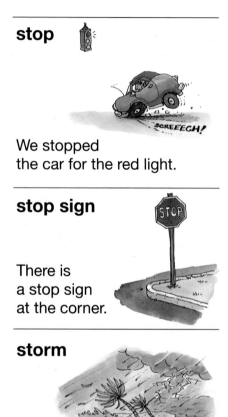

My mom is cooking a sauce on the stove.

straight

Mary's hair is straight.

straw

Steven drinks milk with a straw.

strawberry

We ate strawberries with our ice cream.

stream

Helen and Susan jumped over the stream.

street

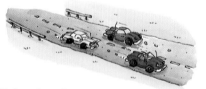

This street is for cars, not trucks.

string

Robert tied the package with string.

stripe

That flag has red and white stripes on it.

stroller

The baby is in the stroller.

strong

Elephants are very strong.

student

The student is writing the alphabet.

submarine

Submarines run under the ocean.

suds

Water and suds spilled on the floor.

sugar

Susan puts sugar on her cereal.

suit

My suit has pants and a jacket.

suitcase

There is space in the suitcase for more shirts.

summer

The weather is hot in the summer.

sun

The sun lights up the Earth.

sunrise

The birds sing at sunrise.

sunset

Winter sunsets can be beautiful.

supermarket

Mom buys our food at the supermarket.

surround

Bushes surround the yard.

swan

Swans live in the pond at the park.

sweater

My grandmother gave me a new sweater.

sweatpants

Thomas received sweatpants for his birthday.

sweatshirt

Mary pulled on her sweatshirt.

sweep*

William is sweeping the floor.

swim*

Helen swims as fast as a fish!

swing

Robert has a swing in his tree.

swing

Steven is swinging on it.

69

Tt *Tt* Tt *Tt*

table

We eat breakfast at the kitchen table.

tablecloth

Mary spread a tablecloth on the table.

tadpole

This tadpole will grow into a frog!

tail

The lion has a very long tail.

take*

Helen took two pieces.

talk

Thomas is talking on the telephone.

tall

One tree is very tall.

target

Helen hit the target with her arrow.

taxi

Robert rode to the airport in a taxi.

tea

My mom drinks her tea with lemon.

teach*

Susan is teaching Mary to play tennis.

teacher

Susan is a good teacher.

team

There are girls and boys on my team.

teeth*

I see your teeth when you smile.

telephone

Mary has a telephone near her bed.

television

Grandpa has a television in his workshop.

tell*

William told his dog to go home.

teller

The teller gave Thomas his money.

tennis

William and Steven are playing tennis.

tennis racket

William is holding his tennis racket.

tent

The girls slept in a large tent.

tentacle

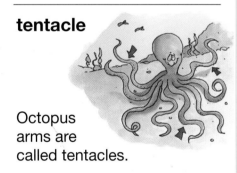

Octopus arms are called tentacles.

terrible

What was that terrible noise?

than

Susan is bigger than Jimmy.

thank you

Thank you for saying "please."

there

Please put it there.

thermometer

The thermometer shows how hot it is.

thin

Helen is too thin to wear my belt.

thing

What is this thing?

think*

Steven is thinking of his birthday.

thread

The thread goes through the eye of the needle.

throne

The king and queen sit on their thrones.

through

William walked through the door.

throw*

Throw the basketball to me.

thumb

Dad hit his thumb with the hammer.

ticket

Thomas has a ticket to see the movie.

tie

The farmer tied
the bull to the fence.

tie

This tie
is for
Dad's birthday.

tiger

Tigers hunt
for food in the jungle.

tightrope

There is a
net under the tightrope.

time

How much
time do you need?

tire

The tires
on this tractor
are as tall as my dad.

to

It is time
to go to bed.

toad

This toad cannot hurt you.

toast

Mary spread
grape jam on her toast.

toaster

Our toaster
has four holes for bread.

toe

People have
five toes on each foot.

together

Susan and
Thomas are
always
together.

toilet

The toilet
is near the sink.

tomato

William cut up
a tomato for the salad.

tongue

William's
tongue is purple.

toolbox

The
carpenter
carries a
toolbox in his truck.

tooth*

The baby has
his first tooth.

toothbrush

The dentist
gave me a new toothbrush.

toothpaste

Jimmy was eating the toothpaste.

top

The top of this table is messy.

top

This top is spinning very fast.

top hat

The dancer is wearing a top hat.

tornado

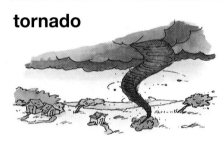

The tornado swept through the town.

towel

Thomas dried the dishes with an old towel.

tower

The castle had a tower at each corner.

town

Our town is very pretty.

toy

The children got out all their toys.

toy store

Mary bought a doll at the toy store.

tractor

The farmer drove the tractor around the field.

traffic jam

There is a traffic jam in the city.

traffic light

Stop when the traffic light is red.

train

The train did not leave on time.

train station

The passengers waited at the train station.

trampoline

The children jump up and down on the trampoline.

trapeze

Susan hangs by her knees on the trapeze.

tray

The waiter carried our food on a tray.

treasure

Steven is digging for treasure on the beach.

tree

There is a tree by the church.

tricycle

Whose tricycle is in the driveway?

trombone

Robert is teaching me to play the trombone.

trophy

Susan won a trophy for being first.

trousers

Dad is wearing his new trousers.

truck

The truck is full of boxes from the factory.

trumpet

The music teacher gave Susan a trumpet.

trunk

The elephant's nose is called a trunk.

trunk

The suitcases are in the trunk of the car.

trunk

The trunk in the attic contains old clothing.

trunks

Robert's trunks are red.

tuba

Thomas sits on a chair to play his tuba.

tugboat

Tugboats push large boats.

tuna

The tuna is a very large fish.

turkey

The turkey is a very large bird.

turtle

Turtles swim in the pond.

tusk

An elephant has two tusks.

tuxedo

My uncle is wearing a tuxedo to the dance.

type

Mary is learning to type.

typewriter

The secretary writes letters on her typewriter.

UuUuUuUu

Uu

umbrella

Steven held the umbrella over us.

umpire

The umpire watches carefully.

uncle

Helen's uncle is her mother's brother.

under

Jimmy is under the table.

underwear

Steven's mom bought him new underwear.

unicorn

The unicorn had a horn on its head.

uniform

Policemen and policewomen wear uniforms.

up

William looked up at the sky.

use

Susan is using her pencil.

use

She is putting it to a good use.

VvVvVvVv

Vv

vacuum cleaner

Mary cleans the rug with the vacuum cleaner.

valley

The valley is between two mountains.

van

The team rides to the game in a van.

vase

There is a vase of flowers on the table.

vegetable

Peas, spinach, and lettuce are green vegetables.

vegetable garden

Grandmother is planting a vegetable garden.

very

YAWN!

William is very tired.

veterinarian

The veterinarian helps sick animals.

village

Susan lives in a small village near the city.

violin

Helen holds the violin under her chin.

volleyball

We played volleyball on the beach.

WwWwWwWw

wade

Thomas isn't swimming. He's wading.

wagon

Helen is pulling a wagon.

waist

Steven has a belt around his waist.

wait

BUS STOP

Mary is waiting for the bus.

waiter

MENU

The waiter gave me a menu.

waiting room

The waiting room is full.

waitress

The waitress filled my glass with water.

walk

Mother walks and the children run.

wall

There is a picture hanging on the wall.

wallet

Dad pulled some money out of his wallet.

walrus

A walrus can swim in cold water.

want

Do you want to read this?

warm

It is warm by the fire.

wash

Susan washed her face and went to bed.

washing machine

Mary's jeans are in the washing machine.

wasp

Wasps built a nest on our porch.

wastebasket

Grandma threw the rags in the wastebasket.

watch

I watch the football game on television.

watch

Robert gave Mom a watch for her birthday.

water
Flowers need water to grow.

water
Helen is watering the flowers.

waterfall

There is a waterfall on the side of the mountain.

watermelon

Aunt Alice cut up the watermelon.

wave

Mary waved to her father.

wave

The wind blows the ocean into waves.

way

This is the way to school.

wear*

People wear clothing, but animals do not.

weather

The weather changes often.

wedding

Helen was in her sister's wedding.

weed

I have to weed the garden!

weed

There are many weeds in my garden.

week

There are seven days in a week.

welcome

We welcomed William to our house.

well

Robert is well.

well

The boys drank water from the well.

wet

Steven's hair is wet.

whale

Whales are very large animals.

what

What is this?

wheat

Flour is made from wheat.

wheel

My bicycle has two wheels.

wheelchair

Aunt Alice uses a wheelchair.

when

When will the alarm clock ring?

where

Where are Susan's shoes?

whistle

He is blowing his whistle.

white

Snowflakes are white.

wide

The river is very wide.

wig

The clown wears a silly orange wig.

win*

Helen won a prize.

wind

The wind blew my hat off.

window

The windows are open in the summer.

wing

Birds use their wings to fly.

winter

Snow covers the ground in winter.

wipe

Susan is wiping the water off her glasses.

with

Mary hit the nail with a hammer.

wolf*

A wolf ran out of the forest.

woman*

My aunt is a short woman.

wood

Robert cut more wood for the fireplace.

woodpecker

A woodpecker makes holes in trees.

word

Mary read the words on the chalkboard.

work

We all work at school.

workshop

Dad fixes things in his workshop.

world

The world is round like a ball.

worm

The bird found a worm in the grass.

wreath

There is a wreath on our door.

wrestling

Robert is on the wrestling team.

wrist

Susan has a bandage on her wrist.

wrench

Dad fixed the faucet with a wrench.

wrinkles

Steven's pants are full of wrinkles.

write*

Some airplanes write in the sky.

XxXxXxXx

xylophone

Helen plays the xylophone.

ZzZzZzZz

zebra

A zebra has black and white stripes.

YyYyYyYy

yarn

The kitten loves to play with yarn.

yellow

The school bus is yellow.

yard

The yard has a fence around it.

yolk

A yolk is the yellow part of an egg.

zipper

Steven's jacket has a long zipper.

zoo

The zoo is my favorite place.

Appendices

Numbers

Days of the Week

Months of the Year

Shapes

Directions

Time

Irregular English Verbs,
Nouns, and Adjectives

Numbers

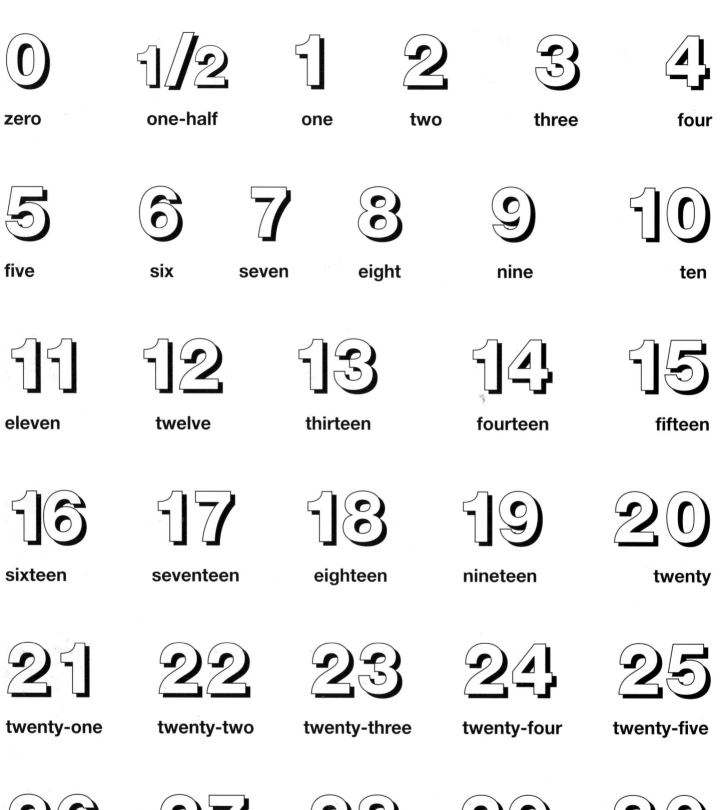

0 zero	**1/2** one-half	**1** one	**2** two	**3** three	**4** four
5 five	**6** six	**7** seven	**8** eight	**9** nine	**10** ten
11 eleven	**12** twelve	**13** thirteen	**14** fourteen	**15** fifteen	
16 sixteen	**17** seventeen	**18** eighteen	**19** nineteen	**20** twenty	
21 twenty-one	**22** twenty-two	**23** twenty-three	**24** twenty-four	**25** twenty-five	
26 twenty-six	**27** twenty-seven	**28** twenty-eight	**29** twenty-nine	**30** thirty	

| thirty-one | thirty-two | thirty-three | thirty-four | thirty-five |

| thirty-six | thirty-seven | thirty-eight | thirty-nine | forty |

| forty-one | forty-two | forty-three | forty-four | forty-five |

| forty-six | forty-seven | forty-eight | forty-nine | fifty |

| fifty-one | fifty-two | fifty-three | fifty-four | fifty-five |

| fifty-six | fifty-seven | fifty-eight | fifty-nine | sixty |

sixty-one   sixty-two   sixty-three   sixty-four   sixty-five

sixty-six   sixty-seven   sixty-eight   sixty-nine   seventy

seventy-one   seventy-two   seventy-three   seventy-four   seventy-five

seventy-six   seventy-seven   seventy-eight   seventy-nine   eighty

eighty-one   eighty-two   eighty-three   eighty-four   eighty-five

eighty-six   eighty-seven   eighty-eight   eighty-nine   ninety

| ninety-one | ninety-two | ninety-three | ninety-four | ninety-five |

| ninety-six | ninety-seven | ninety-eight | ninety-nine |

| one hundred | two hundred | three hundred |

| four hundred | five hundred | one thousand |

ten thousand   one hundred thousand

1,000,000

one million

Days of the Week

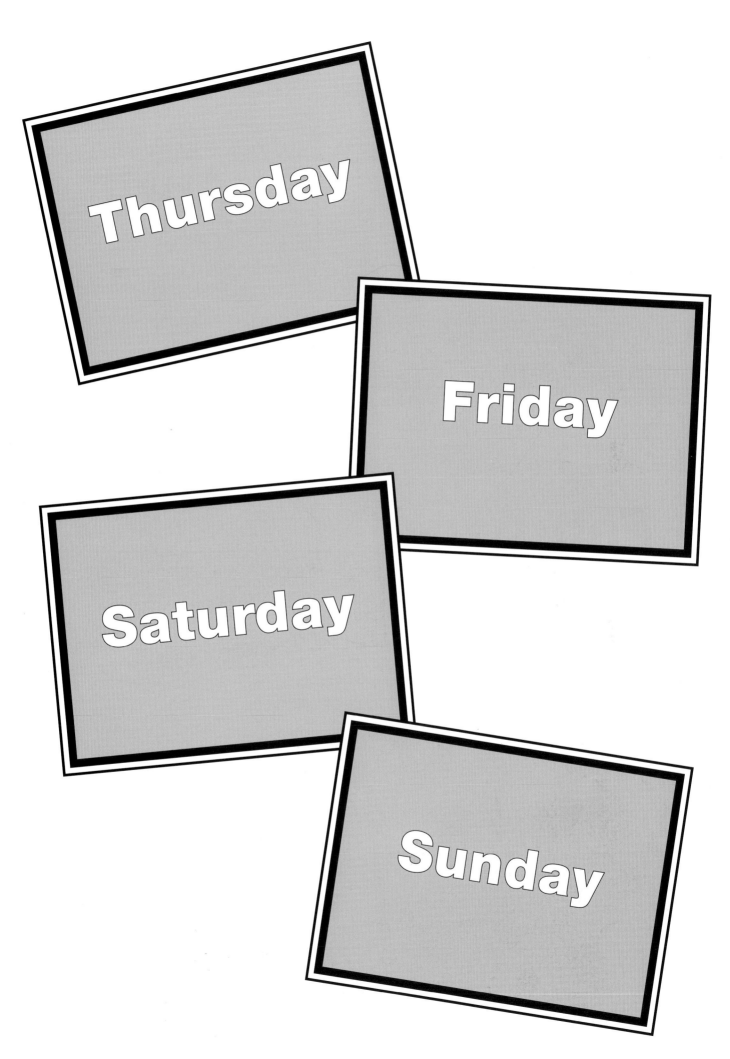

Months of the Year

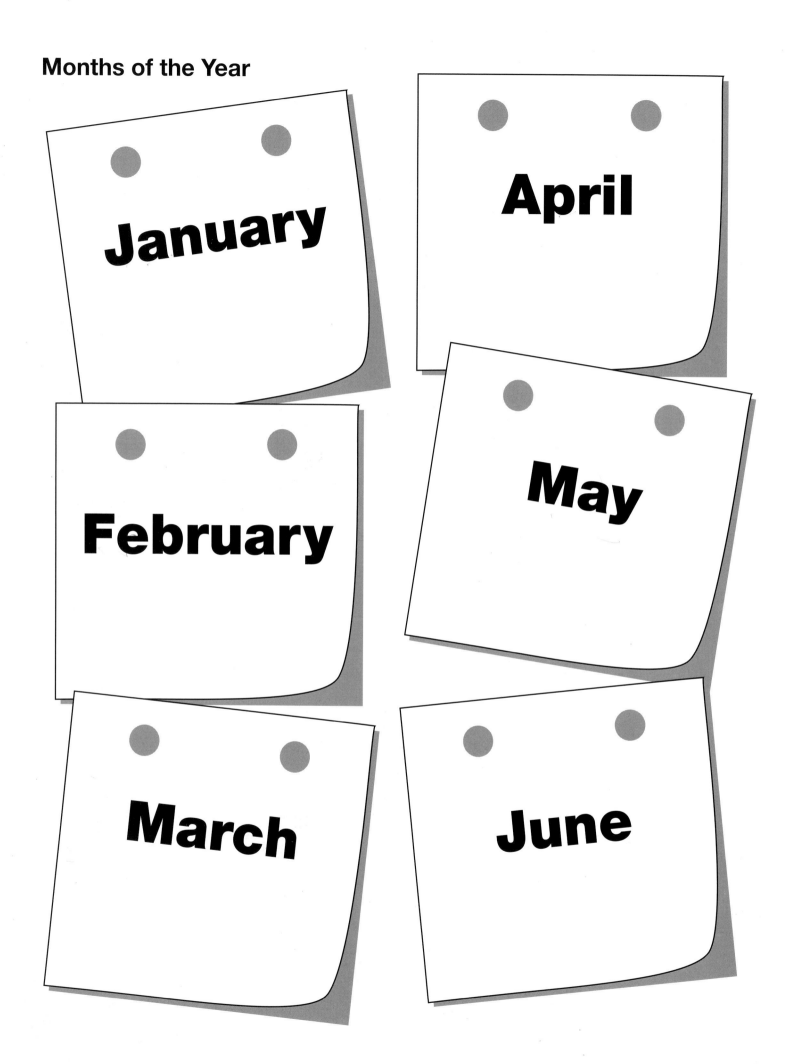

January

April

February

May

March

June

Shapes

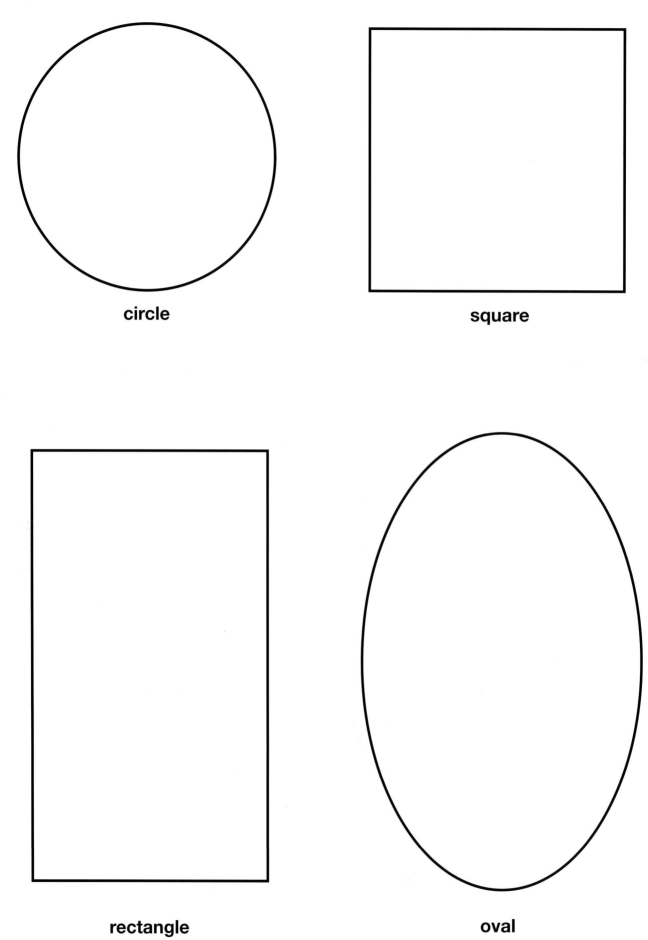

circle

square

rectangle

oval

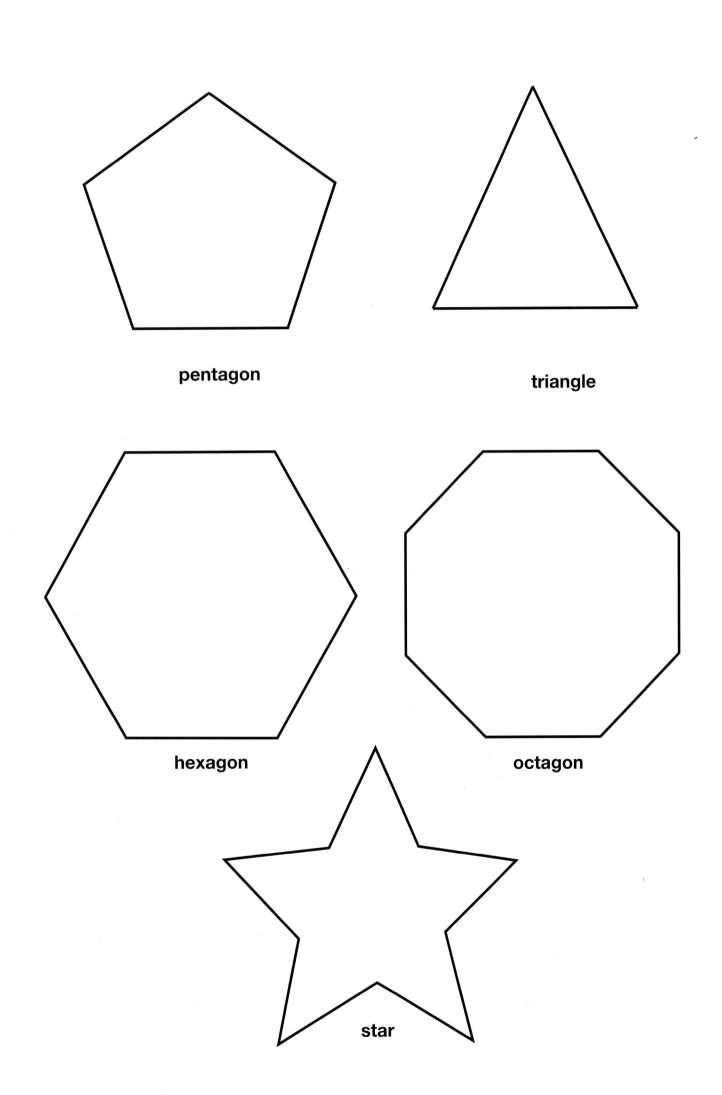

pentagon

triangle

hexagon

octagon

star

Directions

North

South

East

West

Northeast

Northwest

Southeast

Southwest

Time

It is six o'clock.

It is half past six.

It is a quarter of two.

It is midnight.

It is noon.

It is three o'clock.

It is half past four.

It is 1:00 P.M.

It is 1:00 A.M.

Irregular English Verbs

become, became, become
bite, bit, bitten
blow, blew, blown
break, broke, broken
build, built, built
burn, burned or burnt,
  burned
buy, bought, bought
catch, caught, caught
come, came, come
cut, cut, cut
dig, dug, dug
dive, dived or dove, dived
do, did, done
draw, drew, drawn
dream, dreamt or
  dreamed, dreamt or
  dreamed
drink, drank, drunk
drive, drove, driven
eat, ate, eaten
fall, fell, fallen
find, found, found
fly, flew, flown
forget, forgot, forgotten
freeze, froze, frozen
give, gave, given
go, went, gone
grow, grew, grown
hang, hung, hung
have, had, had
hit, hit, hit
hold, held, held
hurt, hurt, hurt
is, was, been (be)

keep, kept, kept
knit, knit or knitted, knit
  or knitted
leap, leapt or leaped, leapt
  or leaped
light, lighted or lit, lighted
  or lit
make, made, made
put, put, put
read, read, read
ride, rode, ridden
ring, rang, rung
run, ran, run
see, saw, seen
sell, sold, sold
sew, sewed, sewn
show, showed, shown
sing, sang, sung
sit, sat, sat
sleep, slept, slept
slide, slid, slid
speak, spoke, spoken
spin, spun, spun
spread, spread, spread
stand, stood, stood
sweep, swept, swept
swim, swam, swum
take, took, taken
teach, taught, taught
tell, told, told
think, thought, thought
throw, threw, thrown
wear, wore, worn
win, won, won
write, wrote, written

Irregular English Nouns

calf, calves
child, children
deer, deer
die, dice
doorman, doormen
fish, fish or fishes
fisherman, fishermen
foot, feet
goose, geese
half, halves
handkerchief,
  handkerchiefs
  or handkerchieves
hoof, hooves
knife, knives
leaf, leaves
man, men
mouse, mice
policeman, policemen
policewoman,
  policewomen
scarf, scarves
sheep, sheep
shelf, shelves
snowman, snowmen
starfish, starfish
tooth, teeth
wolf, wolves
woman, women

Irregular English Adjectives

good, better, best
less, least
more, most